# THE MAGICIAN'

MW01492918

by
C. S. Lewis

## Student Packet

Written by
Debbie Triska Keiser

**Contains masters for:**

|  |  |
|---|---|
| | 3 Prereading Activities |
| | 5 Vocabulary Activities |
| | 1 Study Guide |
| | 7 Literary Analysis Activities |
| | 3 Writing Activities |
| | 2 Critical Thinking Activities |
| | 2 Quizzes |
| | 1 Novel Test |
| | Alternative Assessment |
| **PLUS** | Detailed Answer Key |
| | and Scoring Rubric |

---

### Note

The Harper Trophy paperback edition of the book, published by HarperCollins Publishers, was used to prepare this guide. The page references may differ in other paperback editions.
Novel ISBN: 0-06-447110-1

**Please note:** Parts of this novel deal with sensitive, mature issues. Please assess the appropriateness of this book for the age level and maturity of your students prior to reading and discussing it with them.

---

ISBN 1-58130-860-4

To order, contact your local school supply store, or—
Novel Units, Inc.
P.O. Box 97
Bulverde, TX 78163-0097

Web site: www.educyberstor.com

**Lori Mammen, Editorial Director**
Andrea M. Harris, Production Manager/Production Specialist
Heather Johnson, Product Development Specialist
Suzanne K. Mammen, Curriculum Specialist
Lenella Meister, Production Specialist
Vicky Rainwater, Curriculum Specialist
Jill Reed, Product Development Specialist
Nancy Smith, Product Development Specialist
Adrienne Speer, Production Specialist

Name _____

## Anticipation Guide

**Directions:** Rate each of the following statements before you read the novel and discuss your ratings with a partner. After you have completed the novel, rate and discuss the statements again.

1 ———— 2 ———— 3 ———— 4 ———— 5 ———— 6
strongly agree                                            strongly disagree

|  | Before | After |
|---|---|---|
| 1. Boys and girls can't be good friends. | _____ | _____ |
| 2. Misuse of power for any purpose is wrong. | _____ | _____ |
| 3. Curiosity can have good and bad consequences. | _____ | _____ |
| 4. Selfishness manifests itself in many ways. | _____ | _____ |
| 5. Pride can be good and bad. | _____ | _____ |
| 6. There may be worlds other than our own. | _____ | _____ |
| 7. History has a tendency of repeating itself. | _____ | _____ |
| 8. Power can have positive and negative consequences. | _____ | _____ |
| 9. You can tell a lot about a person by the way he treats an animal. | _____ | _____ |
| 10. Majesty is not determined by blood, but by character. | _____ | _____ |
| 11. Achieving your heart's desire can have both good and bad consequences. | _____ | _____ |
| 12. Evil breeds misery. | _____ | _____ |
| 13. All things are possible when we believe. | _____ | _____ |
| 14. Doing the right thing is sometimes difficult. | _____ | _____ |
| 15. Growing up is full of challenges. | _____ | _____ |

Name _____

**Directions:** Think about each idea listed below. Then freewrite about each idea. Try to write about each idea for at least three minutes. Use extra paper if you need it. Be prepared to discuss your thoughts with classmates.

1. obedience

2. courage

3. magic

4. theft

5. ego

6. selfishness

7. wisdom

8. wickedness

9. power

10. beginning

Name _____

**Directions:** Imagine there are worlds other than our own and you don't have to reach them through space travel. How could we travel there? What might we discover? What might the beings be like who inhabit the new world? Brainstorm, then write for five minutes about the possibilities of new worlds. Use extra paper if you need it.

_____

_____

_____

_____

_____

_____

_____

_____

_____

_____

_____

_____

_____

_____

_____

_____

_____

_____

_____

_____

_____

| indignantly (4) | cistern (6) | pantomime (13) | asylum (19) |
| sages (20) | destiny (21) | ancient (22) | toil (23) |
| preposterous (25) | adept (26) | chivalry (27) | vague (41) |
| solemn (44) | | | |

## Vocabulary Chart

**Directions:** Write each vocabulary word in the left-hand column of the chart. Complete the chart by placing a check mark in the column that best describes your familiarity with each word. Working with a partner, find and read the line where each word appears in the story. Find the meaning of each word in the dictionary. Together with your partner, choose ten of the words checked in the last column. On a separate sheet of paper, use each of those words in a sentence.

| Vocabulary Word | I Can Define | I Have Seen/Heard | New Word For Me |
|---|---|---|---|
|  |  |  |  |
|  |  |  |  |
|  |  |  |  |
|  |  |  |  |
|  |  |  |  |
|  |  |  |  |
|  |  |  |  |
|  |  |  |  |
|  |  |  |  |
|  |  |  |  |
|  |  |  |  |
|  |  |  |  |

Name _____

| extraordinarily (47) | keen (49) | enchantments (53) | despairing (54) |
| obstinate (57) | deplorable (61) | peril (63) | contemptuous (73) |
| minions (75) | deucedly (91) | | |

**Directions:** Locate each word in the story. Use a dictionary to find the definition of the word. Then brainstorm or use a thesaurus to find a synonym and antonym for each word. Fill in the chart below as you work.

**Challenge:** Write each vocabulary word on an index card using pencil. Write each synonym and antonym as well. Shuffle the cards and play a game of "go fish" with a partner. You must have the vocabulary word, its synonym, and antonym in order to "have a match." The person with the most cards at the end of the game is the winner.

| Vocabulary Word | Definition | Synonym | Antonym |
|---|---|---|---|
| | | | |
| | | | |
| | | | |
| | | | |
| | | | |
| | | | |
| | | | |
| | | | |
| | | | |

| | | | |
|---|---|---|---|
| lunged (94) | lunatic (96) | mutton (99) | flogging (101) |
| brandished (110) | compose (111) | delirium (112) | impertinent (116) |
| vivid (119) | lilting (123) | ostentatious (125) | sanatorium (131) |

## Crossword Puzzle

**Directions:** Select ten vocabulary words from above. Create a crossword puzzle answer key by filling in the grid below. Be sure to number the squares for each word. Blacken any spaces not used by the letters. Then, write clues to the crossword puzzle. Number the clues to match the numbers in the squares. The teacher will give each student a blank grid. Make a blank copy of your crossword puzzle for other students to answer. Exchange your clues with someone else and solve the blank puzzle s/he gives you. Check the completed puzzles with the answer keys.

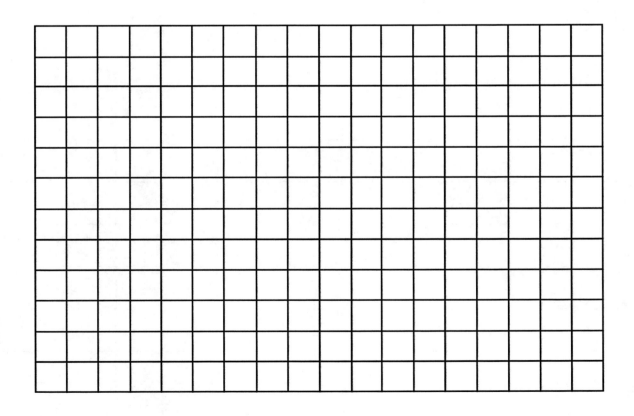

| grave (141) | muddled (145) | vaguely (149) | barred (152) |
| toppled (155) | pardonable (156) | dispute (157) | sagacious (158) |
| revived (158) | astonished (163) | curtsey (164) | abide (165) |
| shied (171) | moorland (174) | upheaval (181) | |

## Vocabulary Cube Pattern

**Directions:** Trace and cut out two vocabulary cube patterns. Choose 12 words from the list and write one word on each side of the cube patterns. Assemble the cubes. Take turns with a partner rolling the cubes and creating sentences using the two words that come up. For example, if you roll "shied" and "upheaval" your sentence might be: The horses *shied* away from the *upheaval* caused by the accident.

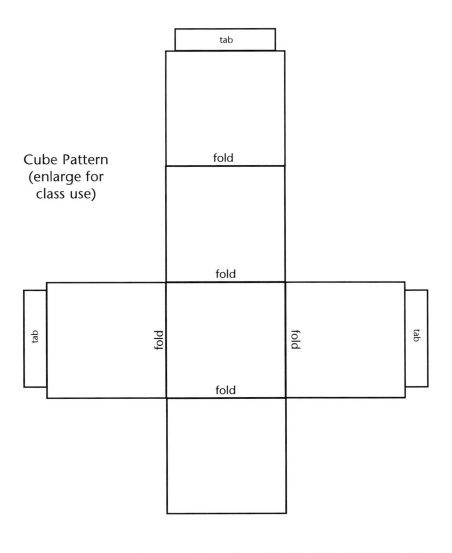

Cube Pattern
(enlarge for
class use)

| | | | |
|---|---|---|---|
| alighted (186) | saffron (190) | counsels (192) | simpleton (192) |
| pitiless (193) | conceited (197) | merciful (204) | solemn (206) |
| loathe (207) | dingy (215) | banisters (217) | trowel (218) |

## Vocabulary Sentence Sets

**Directions:** Choose 10 vocabulary words from the list above. Write the words on the numbered lines below.

1. _____    2. _____

3. _____    4. _____

5. _____    6. _____

7. _____    8. _____

9. _____    10. _____

On a separate sheet of paper, use each of the following sets of words in an original sentence. Your sentences should show that you know the meanings of the vocabulary words as they are used in the story.

Sentence 1: words 8 and 4
Sentence 2: words 9 and 3
Sentence 3: words 1 and 10
Sentence 4: words 7 and 4
Sentence 5: words 3 and 6
Sentence 6: words 5 and 2
Sentence 7: words 7 and 6

## Chapters 1–3, pp. 1–44

1. Do Digory and Polly like one another at first? How can you tell?

2. Why don't you think Polly knows how far the tunnel reaches?

3. What concepts of math do Digory and Polly use to determine how far it will be to the vacant house?

4. Why does Uncle Andrew repeat the word "must" on page 14?

5. Why does Polly begin to change her opinion about Uncle Andrew?

6. What tactic does Uncle Andrew use to quiet Digory after Polly vanishes?

7. How could Uncle Andrew tell the box was magic?

8. How does Digory feel about animals? How can you tell?

9. What reason does Uncle Andrew give Digory for not having tried the experiment himself?

10. What tactic does Uncle Andrew use to get Digory to go after Polly?

11. What words at the top of page 29 let us know Uncle Andrew is uncertain about the outcome of the entire experiment?

12. What reminds Digory and Polly of the reason they are in the Wood Between the Worlds?

13. Why isn't Polly afraid when they can't get back through the original pool?

14. Why do you think Polly's experiment of going only part-way back to their own world might work?

15. Do you think Uncle Andrew saw the children as they came and went back to the Wood Between the Worlds? Explain your answer.

## Chapters 4–6, pp. 45–92

1. Why do you think Digory and Polly hold hands and whisper upon entering the new world?

2. Why is Polly so interested in the people in the room?

3. What starts the argument between Digory and Polly on page 56?

4. What causes the roof to cave in?

5. Why isn't Digory able to hold the Queen's stare?

6. What happens to people who stand in the Queen's way?

7. How does Digory know the sun of Charn is older than the sun of his world?

8. Who does Jadis blame for the destruction of Charn?

9. Why does Jadis look greedy at the mention of a younger world?

10. What happens when Polly and Digory leave Charn?

11. What things doesn't Uncle Andrew understand about the magic rings?

12. Why does Digory hesitate to leave the Queen in the Wood Between the Worlds?

13. What is similar between Jadis and Uncle Andrew's faces?

14. What does the Queen mean when she says "Peace," on pages 83 and 84?

15. Why is Uncle Andrew so interested in dressing up?

## Chapters 7–9, pp. 93–138

1. How does the loss of some power affect the Queen?

2. Why does Digory think it's important to get the Witch back to her own world?

3. What does Jadis do in London?

4. Why does Jadis refer to herself as "we" when she says, "We are the Empress Jadis"?

5. Why is the Queen confused when the people send up cheers, then jeers?

6. What do we learn about the Queen on page 111?

7. What do we see in Uncle Andrew's character as he leaves London and goes to the Wood Between the Worlds?

8. What are some of the Cabby's characteristics?

9. Why does the Witch understand the song better than any of the others?

10. How are the first two songs different?

11. How is Uncle Andrew's selfishness shown on page 125?

12. Why do you think Uncle Andrew and the Witch flee before the Lion?

13. Why doesn't Uncle Andrew like the new world?

14. Why do you think Uncle Andrew forgets about his fear of the Witch when she's not near?

15. What is evident in Uncle Andrew's character when discussing Digory's mother?

16. What happens as the Lion begins singing the wild song?

## Chapters 10–12, pp. 139–181

1. Why do you think Aslan allows some animals to talk and leaves others "dumb"?

2. Which creatures does Aslan choose to help protect Narnia? Why do you think he chose them?

3. What do Strawberry and the Cabby have in common?

4. Why does Strawberry have a difficult time remembering his former life?

5. What does Strawberry remember fondly from his former life?

6. Why does Uncle Andrew try to make himself more stupid?

7. Compare Digory and Uncle Andrew on page 151. Who is really selfish?

8. Why don't the animals realize Uncle Andrew is a creature like the two children and the Cabby?

9. Why do the animals decide to plant Uncle Andrew?

10. Why do the animals think Uncle Andrew is withered and needs water?

11. How does Digory know Aslan isn't satisfied with some of his answers about the Witch?

12. What attributes do we see in Aslan when Digory asks for help for his mother?

13. How does Digory hint for help on his journey?

14. Why don't Fledge, Digory, and Polly complete the journey the first day?

15. What do Digory and Polly do for food during the first night of their journey? the next morning?

16. What do you think Digory, Polly, and Fledge hear in the night?

## Chapters 13–15, pp. 183–221

1. How does the author describe the mood of the garden?

2. Who is watching Digory in the garden?

3. How does the Witch make Digory feel about his mission?

4. What mistake does the Witch make as she tries to convince Digory to take what he wants?

5. Do you think Digory will ever regret his decision not to eat an apple? Why or why not?

6. Why is the mood somber as Digory, Polly, and Fledge make their way back to Narnia?

7. How were the gold and silver trees planted?

8. What did the animals do to make Uncle Andrew's clothes so dirty?

9. What is the only gift Aslan was able to give Uncle Andrew? Did he deserve it?

10. What does Digory admit to Aslan after he tells of the Queen eating an apple?

11. How does Aslan help Digory's mother?

12. What does the reader learn about the difference in the passage of time between Narnia and Digory's world?

13. What is the first thing Uncle Andrew does when he gets home?

14. What happens to the apple core Digory buries in the backyard?

15. What happens to the tree when a storm blows it over?

16. How is the tree connected to Narnia?

## Foreshadowing Chart

**Foreshadowing** is the literary technique of giving clues to coming events in a story.

**Directions:** What examples of foreshadowing do you recall from the story? If necessary, skim through the chapters to find examples of foreshadowing. List at least four examples below. Explain what clues are given, then list the coming event that is suggested.

| Foreshadowing | Page # | Clues | Coming Event |
|---|---|---|---|
|  |  |  |  |
|  |  |  |  |
|  |  |  |  |
|  |  |  |  |
|  |  |  |  |
|  |  |  |  |
|  |  |  |  |
|  |  |  |  |

## Metaphors and Similes

A **metaphor** is a comparison between two unlike objects. For example, "he was a human tree." A **simile** is a comparison between two unlike objects that uses the words *like* or *as*. For example, "the color of her eyes was like the cloudless sky."

**Directions:** Complete the chart below by listing metaphors and similes from the novel, as well as the page numbers on which they are found. Identify metaphors with an "M" and similes with an "S." Translate the comparisons in your own words, and then list the objects being compared.

| Metaphors/Similes | Ideas/Objects Being Compared |
|---|---|
| 1.<br><br>Translation: | |
| 2.<br><br>Translation: | |
| 3.<br><br>Translation: | |

Name _____

**Directions:** Imagine you are one of the "smart animals" in Narnia. Aslan has just told you about the evil that has entered Narnia. Write a newspaper story that one of the animals could have relayed if Narnia had a newspaper.

## The Narnia News

_____

_____

_____

_____

_____

_____

_____

_____

_____

_____

_____

_____

_____

_____

## Protagonists and Antagonists

The main character in a story is called the **protagonist**. Sometimes we call the protagonist the hero or heroine (the "good" person). The character who opposes the hero in a story is called the **antagonist.** Sometimes we call the antagonist the villain (the "bad" person).

**Directions:** Think about stories you have read. Who were some of the protagonists (heroes/heroines) in these stories? Who were the antagonists (villains)? List some of the protagonists and antagonists and the stories in which they appeared.

| Protagonists | Antagonists | Story |
|---|---|---|
| | | |
| | | |
| | | |
| | | |

Complete the charts below by listing some common characteristics of protagonists and antagonists. For example, a protagonist is often brave. An antagonist may be cunning or cruel. Sometimes the antagonist is not just a person but a belief or custom.

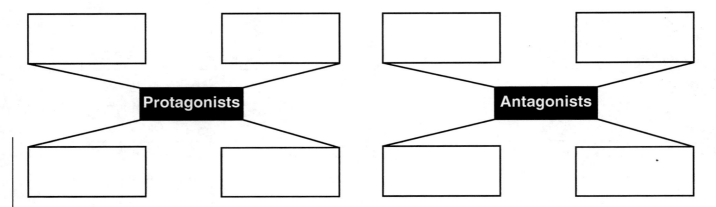

After reading *The Magician's Nephew,* record the protagonist(s) and antagonist(s). Compare and contrast these characters with the characters you listed above.

Name _____

## Who Am I?

**Directions:** Write a riddle describing a character in the novel. Include adjectives, adverbs, nouns, and verbs that will help other students see this character in their mind's eye. Describe how the person looks, acts, feels, talks, and how other people in the story treat this character. (Do not reveal which character is the answer to your riddle.)

---

**Who am I?**

**I have**

_____

_____

_____

**I can**

_____

_____

_____

**In the story, people say I** _____

_____

_____

---

## Bio-poem

**Directions:** Digory is a very strong character in *The Magician's Nephew*. As the story goes on, Digory becomes more responsible for his behavior and begins to realize there are consequences, both good and bad, for his and others' actions. What kind of person is Digory at the end of the book? Is he a character you admire? Using the format below, write a bio-poem about Digory Kirke. After you have written a bio-poem about Digory, write a bio-poem about yourself using the same format.

—Line  1:  First name only
—Line  2:  Lover of (list three things character loves)
—Line  3:  Giver of (list three things character gives)
—Line  4:  Needs (list three things character needs)
—Line  5:  Wants (list three things character wants)
—Line  6:  Is good at (list three things character is good at)
—Line  7:  Should work on (list three things character needs to improve)
—Line  8:  Is similar to (list three people or other characters to whom this character is similar and list a reason behind each character)
—Line  9:  Survivor of (list three things the character survives)
—Line 10:  Last name only

Title _____

1. _____

2. _____

3. _____

4. _____

5. _____

6. _____

7. _____

8. _____

9. _____

10. _____

Name _____

# Story Map

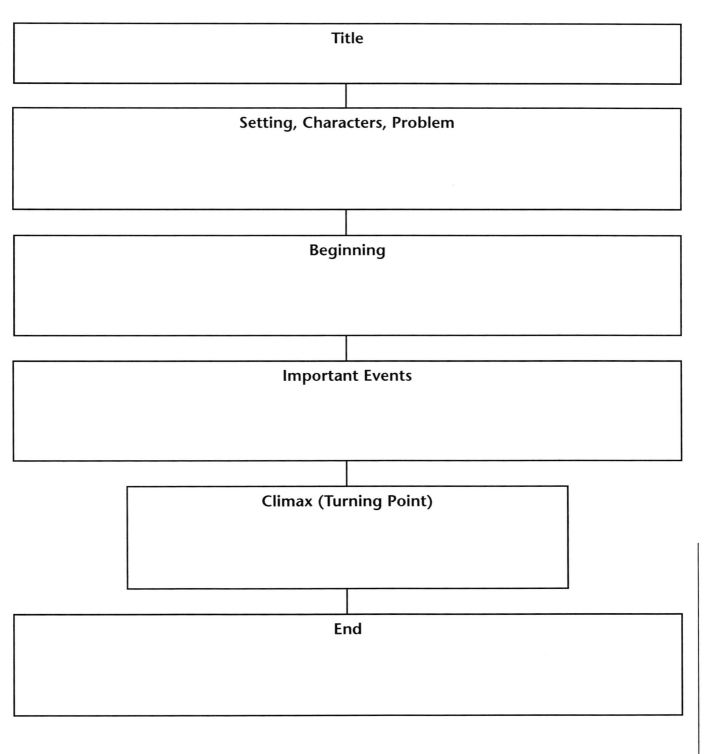

**Title**

**Setting, Characters, Problem**

**Beginning**

**Important Events**

**Climax (Turning Point)**

**End**

## Idioms, Onomatopoeias, and Oxymorons! Oh My!

**Idioms** are words or groups of words that can't be understood by their literal meaning. Instead of simply saying, "I'm in trouble," we might use an idiomatic expression, "I'm in the doghouse." People who learn English as a second language have a difficult time learning our idiomatic expressions, just as it is difficult for English speakers to learn foreign idioms.

**Onomatopoeias** (on-oh-mot-oh-pee-uhs) are words that resemble the sounds they refer to, such as *pop* or *bang*.

**Oxymorons** are words used together that clash with one another, such as *never again*, *found missing*, and *sun shade*.

**Directions:** C. S. Lewis employs many literary devices in his writing. Search through *The Magician's Nephew* looking for idioms, onomatopoeias, and oxymorons. Record each example you find with the corresponding page number below.

| Idioms | Onomatopoeias | Oxymorons |
|---|---|---|
| "Polly's heart came into her mouth," p. 14 | "plop-plop," p. 134 | "jolly rotten," p. 20 |
| | | |
| | | |
| | | |
| | | |
| | | |
| | | |
| | | |

## Story Pyramid

**Directions:** Using the pyramid, write words or phrases to summarize the story.

Line 1: One word that gives the setting

Line 2: Two words that identify the two main characters (in order of their appearance)

Line 3: Three words that explain the problem

Line 4: Two words that describe character #1; two words that describe character #2

Line 5: Two characters that interact with character #1; three characters that interact with character #2

Line 6: Six words that explain the resolution of the conflict

Line 7: Seven words that summarize your impression of the book

1 _____

2 _____ _____

3 _____ _____ _____

4 _____ _____ _____ _____

5 _____ _____ _____ _____ _____

6 _____ _____ _____ _____ _____ _____

7 _____ _____ _____ _____ _____ _____ _____

Name _____

# Understanding Values

**Values** represent people's beliefs about what is important, good, or worthwhile. For example, most families value spending time together.

**Directions:** Think about the following characters from *The Magician's Nephew*. What do they value? What beliefs do they have about what is important, good, or worthwhile? On the chart below, list each character's three most important values, from most important to least. Be prepared to share your lists during a class discussion.

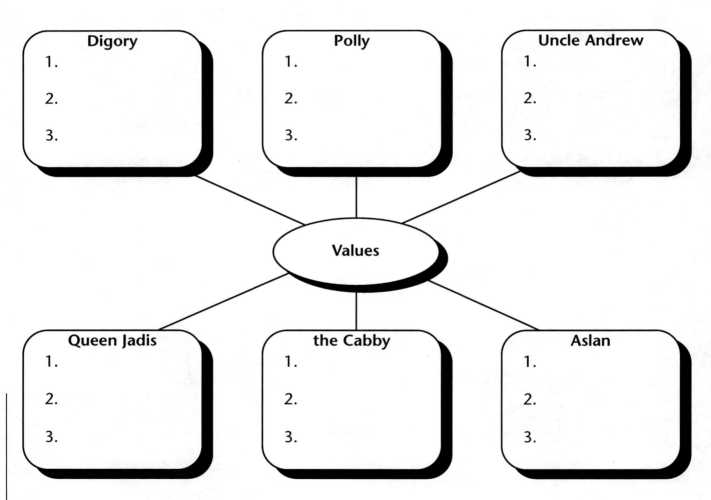

**Digory**
1.
2.
3.

**Polly**
1.
2.
3.

**Uncle Andrew**
1.
2.
3.

**Values**

**Queen Jadis**
1.
2.
3.

**the Cabby**
1.
2.
3.

**Aslan**
1.
2.
3.

After you have finished the chart and participated in the class discussion, think about which character seems to have values most like your own. Write a paragraph that explains why you chose this character.

Name _____

## Cause/Effect Map

**Directions:** List events from the story that cause Digory's character to change throughout the novel.

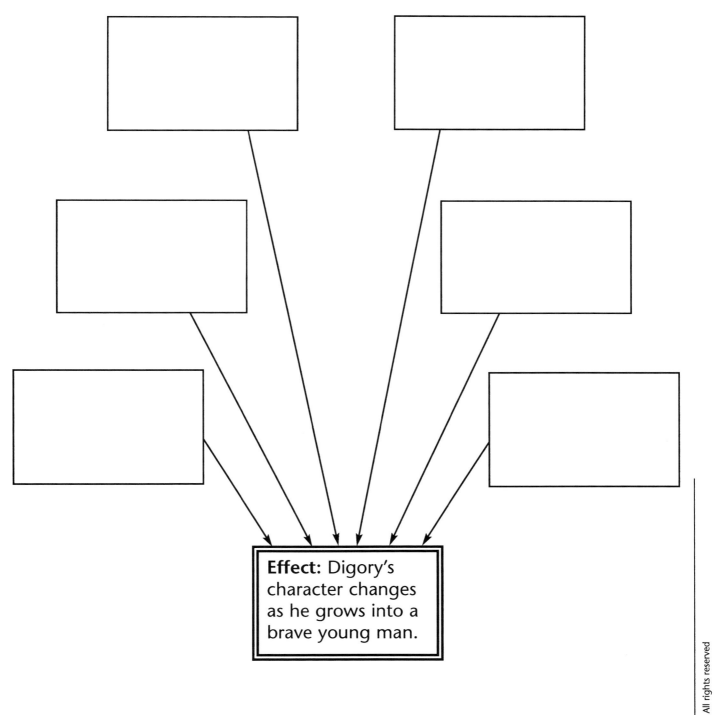

**Effect:** Digory's character changes as he grows into a brave young man.

Name _____

**Directions:** Identify each of the following words and explain the importance of each to the story.

1. selfishness

   _____

2. Narnia

   _____

3. courage

   _____

4. responsibility

   _____

5. curiosity

   _____

6. evil

   _____

7. obedience

   _____

8. ceremony

   _____

9. life

   _____

10. blessings

    _____

**Directions:** Write a brief answer for each question.

1. How do Digory and Polly meet?

2. Why do Digory and Polly become friends?

3. How does Uncle Andrew trick Polly into putting on a ring?

4. Where does Digory find Polly when he puts on a ring?

5. What happens when Digory strikes the bell with the hammer?

6. How can the children tell that Jadis is from another race?

7. How were all the people of Charn destroyed?

8. What problem arises when the children leave Charn?

9. What reaction does Queen Jadis have to the Wood Between the Worlds?

10. How does Uncle Andrew react when he sees the Queen?

11. What does Uncle Andrew do to try to satisfy Jadis?

12. How does Jadis cause a scene in London?

13. Who pursues Jadis as she tears through the streets of London?

14. Who is the only person who genuinely tries to help the situation?

Name _____

**Directions:** Choose the BEST answer.

_____ 1. What do the people do as Jadis shouts about being an empress?
    A. mob her
    B. ask for autographs
    C. call for more police
    D. mock her

_____ 2. What do Digory and Polly do to help the situation?
    A. They catch the Queen and take her to the Wood Between the Worlds.
    B. They catch the Queen and take her back to Charn.
    C. They catch the Queen and take her to a new world.
    D. They leave and pretend they don't know how the Queen got there.

_____ 3. Who ends up in the Wood Between the Worlds?
    A. Polly, Digory, and Jadis
    B. Polly and Digory
    C. Polly, Digory, Uncle Andrew, Jadis, Strawberry, and the Cabby
    D. Polly, Digory, and Strawberry

_____ 4. Who has a positive attitude when they reach the place that is "uncommonly like Nothing"?
    A. Polly
    B. Digory
    C. the Cabby
    D. Uncle Andrew

_____ 5. What is the purpose of the Voice?
    A. to create night and day
    B. to create the stars
    C. to create the plants and animals
    D. All of the above.

_____ 6. What effect does the Voice have on Uncle Andrew and Jadis?
    A. They love the beautiful Voice.
    B. The Voice makes them want to play and frolic.
    C. The Voice makes them feel weak and ill.
    D. The Voice makes them feel important.

_____ 7. Who argues about going back to their own world?
    A. Polly and Digory
    B. the Cabby and Uncle Andrew
    C. the Cabby and Jadis
    D. Uncle Andrew and Jadis

_____ 8. Why does Uncle Andrew suddenly change his mind about the value of the new world?
    A. He wishes to live there with the beautiful trees.
    B. He sees the lamppost grow into a tree and wonders if he could grow trees of iron.
    C. He wishes to rule the new world as king with Jadis.
    D. He wants to put the animals to work for him.

_____ 9. What ability does Aslan bestow upon some of the animals he creates?
    A. read minds
    B. run fast
    C. read
    D. talk

_____ 10. What is the evil of which Aslan speaks?
    A. leprechauns
    B. Digory
    C. wolves
    D. Queen Jadis

_____ 11. What does Strawberry become?
    A. a talking horse
    B. a flying horse
    C. a flying donkey
    D. both A and B

_____ 12. Why do the animals think Uncle Andrew is a tree?
    A. He doesn't talk.
    B. He looks different than the other humans.
    C. He doesn't move.
    D. All of the above.

_____ 13. Who does Digory see when he goes to the garden?
A. Queen Jadis
B. Aslan
C. the Cabby
D. Uncle Andrew

_____ 14. What precious gift does Aslan give Digory?
A. a golden medal
B. freedom
C. a healing apple for his mother
D. the ability to see the future

_____ 15. What do Polly and Digory do to prevent Uncle Andrew from going back to Narnia?
A. They move the Wood Between the Worlds.
B. They sing a song to permanently close the door to Narnia forever.
C. They ask Aslan to lock the door to Narnia.
D. They bury the rings where no one will ever find them.

**A. Matching:** Match each character with the correct description.

| | | |
|---|---|---|
| ____ | 1. Digory | A. powerful, omniscient, loving |
| ____ | 2. Polly | B. evil, huge, strong |
| ____ | 3. Uncle Andrew | C. courageous, young, curious |
| ____ | 4. Queen Jadis | D. hard-working, helpful, able to fly |
| ____ | 5. the Cabby | E. conniving, selfish, wimpy |
| ____ | 6. Aslan | F. practical, thankful, caring |
| ____ | 7. Fledge | G. curious, creative, thoughtful |

**B. Quotations:** Match the name of the character to the correct quotation.

A. Digory  B. Polly  C. Uncle Andrew  D. Jadis  E. Aslan  F. the Cabby  G. Fledge

____ 8. "Come on little one, I've had things like you on my back before."

____ 9. "Why haven't these clothes all rotted away long ago?"

____ 10. "We shall always be wondering what else would have happened if we had struck the bell."

____ 11. "She was my godmother. That's her, there, on the wall."

____ 12. "I'd ha' been a better man all my life if I'd known there were things like this."

____ 13. "You are a very naughty and impertinent little boy."

____ 14. "There is an evil Witch abroad in my new land of Narnia."

____ 15. "This is not Charn. This is an empty world."

**C. Graphic Organizer:** List three problems that Digory faces throughout the story on the chart below.

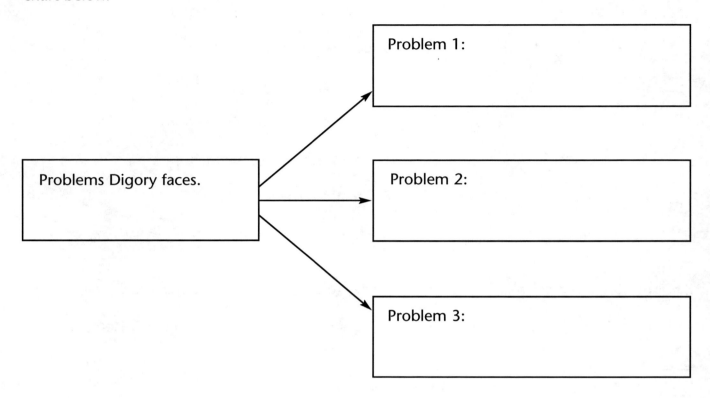

**D. Open-Ended Prompt:** Throughout the story Digory makes decisions that require much thought and wisdom. Write a paragraph explaining how Digory changes as he grows into a brave young man in the book. Use examples to support your ideas.

_____

_____

_____

_____

_____

_____

_____

_____

_____

_____

Name _____

## Creative Writing Alternative Assessment

**Directions**: Select one of the following topics and write an essay on the lines below.

A. Imagine that Digory, Polly, and Uncle Andrew never returned from Narnia. How might the story have been different? Write a new ending to the book in which they choose to stay and help rule Narnia. Use language from the book and be descriptive.

B. Imagine that Digory and Polly had not buried the rings as Aslan asked them to do at the end of the story. What adventures might they have had? Brainstorm and write an adventure Polly and Digory could have shared after another trip to the Wood Between the Worlds. What world would they discover? How old would it be? Who or what would live there? Be descriptive and creative.

_____

_____

_____

_____

_____

_____

_____

_____

_____

_____

_____

_____

_____

_____

_____

_____

_____

_____

# Answer Key

**Activities #1–#4:** Answers will vary.

**Activity #5:** Answers may vary, but suggested answers include: extraordinarily: amazingly, ordinarily; keen: enthusiastic, apathetic; enchantments: magic, commonplace; despairing: pessimistic, hopeful; obstinate: closed-minded, pliable; deplorable: dire, beneficial; peril: danger, safety; contemptuous: distasteful, tasteful; minions: underlings, bosses; deucedly: extremely, moderately

**Activities #6–#8:** Answers will vary.

**Study Guide**

**Chapters 1–3:** 1. No. They are short with one another, and they argue (pp. 2–3). 2. She never explored very far by herself (p. 7). 3. addition, multiplication, non-standard measurement, estimation (p. 8) 4. He is questioning Digory's tone and considers it disrespectful (p. 14). 5. He flatters her by saying she's "an attractive young lady" (p. 15). 6. He reminds Digory that he might disturb his ailing mother (p. 17). 7. He felt it pricking his fingers (p. 20). 8. He likes animals because he becomes upset over Uncle Andrew using guinea pigs in his experiments (p. 24). 9. He says he is too old to survive a dangerous trip to another world (pp. 25–26). 10. He makes reference to Digory being a coward (p. 27). 11. "hasn't been tested yet, but I expect" (p. 29) 12. They see the guinea pig with a yellow ring attached and gradually remember why they are there (p. 35). 13. The wood is a peaceful place, and no one can really be upset there (p. 37). 14. She remembers coming into this world through the pool slowly and assumes the trip back will be just as slow (pp. 39–40). 15. Answers will vary (p. 41).

**Chapters 4–6:** 1. They are nervous and don't know who might be watching them (p. 47). 2. She is interested in their clothes (p. 52). 3. Digory wants to ring the bell, and Polly doesn't think it's a good idea (p. 56). 4. either the magic or the loud sound of the bell (p. 59) 5. He knows she is more powerful than he (p. 63). 6. They are destroyed (p. 67). 7. It doesn't shine as brightly (p. 68). 8. her sister (p. 69) 9. She thinks about taking over the world Digory and Polly came from (p. 72). 10. Jadis grabs Polly's hair and comes to the Wood Between the Worlds with them (p. 77). 11. You don't have to be touching a ring, only touching someone who has a ring, to move between the worlds. The green rings are for getting to the Wood Between the Worlds only. The yellow rings take wearers to different worlds (p. 78). 12. He is torn between the Queen's beauty and Polly's insistence that they leave her (p. 79). 13. their expressions (p. 80) 14. Be quiet (pp. 83–84). 15. He wants to impress the Queen (p. 88).

**Chapters 7–9:** 1. She doesn't lose her nerve (p. 94). 2. She is dangerous, and he doesn't want her to bother his sick mother (p. 96). 3. She steals jewelry and a cab (pp. 101–104). 4. Answers will vary (p. 107). 5. She is not used to being mocked as she is all-powerful in Charn (p. 109). 6. She has destroyed many other worlds besides Charn (p. 111). 7. He is a great, whiny coward (pp. 111–112). 8. kind, caring, logical, religious (pp. 114–115) 9. She hears the peace in the song, and doesn't like it because it goes against her values. She understands that there is something more powerful than she (pp. 118–119). 10. The first song had to be more powerful to create stars and the sun; the new song is more gentle to create vegetation (p. 123). 11. All of his complaints are about himself and how he has been treated (p. 125). 12. The Lion represents goodness, and Uncle Andrew and the Witch are evil. Evil cannot stand in the face of good (p. 128). 13. He is concerned about the state of his clothing and has no interest in what is happening (p. 129). 14. The Witch is so beautiful that the memory of her is jaded by her beauty (p. 130). 15. He does not care for anyone but himself (p. 132). 16. Animals spring forth from the ground (pp. 133–135).

**Chapters 10–12:** 1. Answers will vary (p. 140). 2. Dwarf, River-god, Oak, He-Owl, both Ravens, Bull-Elephant; Answers will vary (p. 142). 3. They both prefer the country (p. 146). 4. He has been given knowledge and the ability to speak (p. 145). 5. sugar cube treats (p. 147) 6. He can't handle the fact that the animals in this world can talk and sing. He wants to be ignorant of it all (p. 150). 7. Answers will vary; Uncle Andrew (p. 151) 8. They don't understand clothes yet, all have on different kinds of clothing, and Uncle Andrew can't talk (p. 153). 9. They listed his attributes and decided he must be a tree that needed planting (p. 157). 10. He is old and wrinkled. His clothes are wrinkled, too (p. 158). 11. Aslan pauses when he knows details have been left out of Digory's answers (pp. 160–161). 12. grief, compassion, wisdom (p. 168) 13. He tells Aslan the journey will take awhile (p. 170). 14. They start their journey in the middle of the first day, and it is too far to reach that day (pp. 173–177). 15. They eat leftover toffee from Polly's pocket and plant one piece in the ground. The next morning they enjoy toffee-flavored fruit from the new tree that has grown (pp. 179–180). 16. Answers will vary (p. 181).

**Chapters 13–15:** 1. happy, but serious (p. 188) 2. the bird and the Witch (p. 190) 3. sad, confused (p. 193) 4. She mentions leaving Polly behind (p. 194). 5. Answers will vary (pp. 195–196). 6. They don't know what to say to Digory after everything the Witch said to make him feel bad (pp. 195–196). 7. when change fell out of Uncle Andrew's pocket (pp. 199–204) 8. The animals were caring for the creature the best they knew how. They weren't trying to harm him (p. 201). 9. sleep; no (p. 203) 10. He almost ate an apple (p. 208). 11. He tells Digory to take an apple from the tree and feed it to his mother (p. 209). 12. Time doesn't progress in Digory's world when he visits Narnia (p. 213). 13. gets a drink of brandy (p. 214) 14. It grows into a tree (pp. 216–217). 15. Digory has the timber made into a wardrobe (p. 220). 16. In the future, people discover a way to use the wardrobe to go between their world and Narnia (pp. 220–221).

**Activities #9–#20:** Answers will vary.

**Quiz #1:** 1. They meet when Digory climbs over the wall of the garden. 2. They are bored because of bad weather outside, so they spend a lot of time playing inside. 3. He tells her he wants to give her a present. 4. the Wood Between the Worlds 5. He awakens the evil Queen Jadis. 6. She is much taller and stronger than all humans they know. 7. Queen Jadis used the Deplorable Word and destroyed Charn. 8. Queen Jadis leaves Charn with them. 9. She becomes weak and ill. 10. He is taken with her beauty and frightened of her strength and power. 11. He hires a cab to take her through London. 12. She steals jewelry, takes control of a hansom, and rides wildly through the streets back to Digory's house. 13. policemen, commoners, errand boys, and the Cabby 14. the Cabby

**Quiz #2:** 1. D 2. A 3. C 4. C 5. D 6. C 7. D 8. B 9. D 10. D 11. D 12. D 13. A 14. C 15. D

**Novel Test: A.** 1. C 2. G 3. E 4. B 5. F 6. A 7. D **B.** 8. G (p. 172) 9. B (p. 53) 10. A (p. 56) 11. C (p. 18) 12. F (p. 117) 13. C (p. 116) 14. E (p. 160) 15. D (p. 113) **C.** Answers will vary. **D.** Refer to the rubric on p. 36 of this guide.

**Alternative Assessment:** Answers will vary.

# Linking Novel Units® Student Packets to National and State Reading Assessments

During the past several years, an increasing number of students have faced some form of state-mandated competency testing in reading. Many states now administer state-developed assessments to measure the skills and knowledge emphasized in their particular reading curriculum. This Novel Units® guide includes open-ended comprehension questions that correlate with state-mandated reading assessments. The rubric below provides important information for evaluating responses to open-ended comprehension questions. Teachers may also use scoring rubrics provided for their own state's competency test.

## Scoring Rubric for Open-Ended Items

**3-Exemplary**
Thorough, complete ideas/information
Clear organization throughout
Logical reasoning/conclusions
Thorough understanding of reading task
Accurate, complete response

**2-Sufficient**
Many relevant ideas/pieces of information
Clear organization throughout most of response
Minor problems in logical reasoning/conclusions
General understanding of reading task
Generally accurate and complete response

**1-Partially Sufficient**
Minimally relevant ideas/information
Obvious gaps in organization
Obvious problems in logical reasoning/conclusions
Minimal understanding of reading task
Inaccuracies/incomplete response

**0-Insufficient**
Irrelevant ideas/information
No coherent organization
Major problems in logical reasoning/conclusions
Little or no understanding of reading task
Generally inaccurate/incomplete response